**DATE DUE**

U.S. WARS

# THE FRENCH
## AND
# INDIAN WAR

## A MyReportLinks.com Book

Carl R. Green

MyReportLinks.com Books

an imprint of

**Enslow Publishers, Inc.**
Box 398, 40 Industrial Road
Berkeley Heights, NJ 07922
USA

MyReportLinks.com Books, an imprint of Enslow Publishers, Inc.

**Library of Congress Cataloging-in-Publication Data**

Green, Carl R.
  The French and Indian War / Carl R. Green.
    p. cm. — (U.S. wars)
  Summary: Discusses the major battles, military tactics, and famous
figures of this war rooted in European rivalries and fought in the Ohio
Valley wilderness. Includes Internet links to related Web sites, source
documents, and photographs.
  Includes bibliographical references (p.   ) and index.
  ISBN 0-7660-5090-4
  1. United States—History—French and Indian War, 1755–1763—Juvenile
literature. [1. United States—History—French and Indian War,
1755–1763.] I. Title. II. Series.
  E199 .G76 2002
  973.2'6—dc21
                                    2001008194

Printed in the United States of America

10 9 8 7 6 5 4 3 2

**To Our Readers:**
Through the purchase of this book, you and your library gain access to the Report Links that specifically
back up this book.
The Publisher will provide access to the Report Links that back up this book and will keep these Report
Links up to date on **www.myreportlinks.com** for three years from the book's first publication date.
We have done our best to make sure all Internet addresses in this book were active and appropriate when we
went to press. However, the author and the Publisher have no control over, and assume no liability for, the
material available on those Internet sites or on other Web sites they may link to.
The usage of the MyReportLinks.com Books Web site is subject to the terms and conditions stated on the
Usage Policy Statement on **www.myreportlinks.com**.
In the future, a password may be required to access the Report Links that back up this book. The password
is found on the bottom of page 4 of this book.
Any comments or suggestions can be sent by e-mail to comments@myreportlinks.com or to the address on
the back cover.

**Photo Credits:** © Corel Corporation, pp. 1 (background), 3; Courtesy of Digital History, p. 36;
Courtesy of MyReportLinks.com Books, p. 4; Courtesy of Ohio History Central, pp. 17, 18, 42;
Courtesy of Rearview Mirror: *The Detroit News*, pp. 26, 40; Courtesy of Significant Scots, pp. 21;
Courtesy of The Battle of the Restigouche, p. 29; Courtesy of The Point, p. 31; Enslow Publishers,
pp. 13, 32, 35, 38; Library of Congress, p. 11; Painting by Don Troiani, www.historicalprints.com.

**Cover Photo:** Painting by Don Troiani, www.historicalprints.com.

**Cover Description:** Battle of Bushy Run

# Contents

# MyReportLinks.com Books
## Great Books, Great Links, Great for Research!

MyReportLinks.com Books present the information you need to learn about your report subject. In addition, they show you where to go on the Internet for more information. The pre-evaluated Report Links that back up this book are kept up to date on **www.myreportlinks.com**. With the purchase of a MyReportLinks.com Books title, you and your library gain access to the Report Links that specifically back up that book. The Report Links save hours of research time and link to dozens—even hundreds—of Web sites, source documents, and photos related to your report topic.

Please see "To Our Readers" on the Copyright page for important information about this book, the MyReportLinks.com Books Web site, and the Report Links that back up this book.

**Access:**

The Publisher will provide access to the Report Links that back up this book and will try to keep these Report Links up to date on our Web site for three years from the book's first publication date. Please enter **AFI1847** if asked for a password.

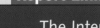

**Report Links**

The Internet sites described below can be accessed at
**http://www.myreportlinks.com**

*EDITOR'S CHOICE

▶**Maps of the French and Indian War**
At this Web site you will find a brief history of the French and Indian
War, maps, and an online atlas.

Link to this Internet site from http://www.myreportlinks.com

*EDITOR'S CHOICE

▶**The French & Indian War 1754–1763**
This Web site provides a brief overview of the French and Indian War.
You will also find links to information about George Washington, Fort
Necessity, Fort Duquesne, and the Treaty of Paris.

Link to this Internet site from http://www.myreportlinks.com

*EDITOR'S CHOICE

▶**The French and Indian War**
At this Web site you will find a detailed account of key events during
the French and Indian War. You will also find a helpful glossary of
eighteenth century military terms.

Link to this Internet site from http://www.myreportlinks.com

*EDITOR'S CHOICE

▶**Treaty of Paris, 1763**
The site contains the text of the Treaty of Paris in French and English.
This treaty ended the Seven Years' War between France and Britain.

Link to this Internet site from http://www.myreportlinks.com

*EDITOR'S CHOICE

▶**George Washington the Soldier**
America's Story from America's Library, a Library of Congress Web site,
provides a brief overview of George Washington's role in the French
and Indian War. Here you will learn about the battles he fought and
how he rose to the rank of brigadier general.

Link to this Internet site from http://www.myreportlinks.com

*EDITOR'S CHOICE

▶**Archiving Early America**
By navigating through this Web site you can explore Colonial America.
Here you will find important documents and events that occurred
during the Colonial period.

Link to this Internet site from http://www.myreportlinks.com

**Report Links**

## The Internet sites described below can be accessed at http://www.myreportlinks.com

### ▶ The Battle of the Restigouche
This site provides a detailed account of the last naval engagement of the Seven Years' War between Britain and France. Fought in the Restigouche River, the battle kept the French fleet and reinforcements from reaching New France and ultimately determined the outcome of the war.

*Link to this Internet site from http://www.myreportlinks.com*

### ▶ Braddock's Defeat
This site holds a letter written by twenty-three year old George Washington, describing the battle in which he fought against the French under General Braddock. The general's combined force of British soldiers and colonial militiamen were defeated in the battle.

*Link to this Internet site from http://www.myreportlinks.com*

### ▶ Colonial America (1492–1763)
America's Story from America's Library, a Library of Congress Web site, provides a brief history of Colonial America from 1492 through 1763. You will also find links to more information about Colonial America.

*Link to this Internet site from http://www.myreportlinks.com*

### ▶ FAS Military Analysis Network: French and Indian War
This brief essay provides an excellent overview of the French and Indian War. It explores the tensions that existed between Europe's three major colonial powers and how they sparked a series of conflicts, that led to the French and Indian War.

*Link to this Internet site from http://www.myreportlinks.com*

### ▶ Fighting for a Continent
At this site you will read newspaper articles of the time period, covered by the French and Indian War. The newspapers include five colonial periodicals from Maryland, Massachusetts, New York, Pennsylvania, and South Carolina.

*Link to this Internet site from http://www.myreportlinks.com*

### ▶ The Fort Edwards Web Page
At this Web site you will find the history of Fort Edwards. Here you will learn about the building of the fort, the battle of Great Cacapon, and the French and Indian War.

*Link to this Internet site from http://www.myreportlinks.com*

Any comments? Contact us: **comments@myreportlinks.com**

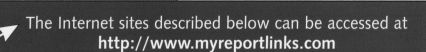
The Internet sites described below can be accessed at
http://www.myreportlinks.com

▶**Fort Necessity**
At the National Park Service Web site you can visit Fort Necessity and
learn about its role in the French and Indian War. Here you will find a
general overview of the fort and a link to more detailed information
about Fort Necessity and the war.

Link to this Internet site from http://www.myreportlinks.com

▶**The Fort at No. 4**
This site provides an introduction to the Fort at No. 4, one of the
northernmost of the British settlements on the Connecticut River. A
fortified village, it figured prominently in the French and Indian War.

Link to this Internet site from http://www.myreportlinks.com

▶**Fort Ticonderoga National Historic Landmark**
The official Web site of the Fort Ticonderoga National Historic
Landmark recalls the stunning French victories at the fort during the
French and Indian War. The photo gallery contains photographs of
the fort, artifacts, and reenactments.

Link to this Internet site from http://www.myreportlinks.com

▶**Fortress of Louisbourg National Historic Site of Canada**
This site provides a brief history of the Fortress of Louisbourg used by
the French during the French and Indian War. In 1758, the fortress
was captured by British troops and demolished.

Link to this Internet site from http://www.myreportlinks.com

▶**French and Indian War**
Britannica Intermediate provides a brief history of the French and
Indian War. Here you will learn about the key combatants, major
battles, causes, and outcome.

Link to this Internet site from http://www.myreportlinks.com

▶**French and Indian War**
Encyclopedia.com provides a brief overview of the French and Indian
War. You will also find a link to more information about the war and
key events.

Link to this Internet site from http://www.myreportlinks.com

**Report Links**

 The Internet sites described below can be accessed at
http://www.myreportlinks.com

▶**French and Indian War**

At this site you will find an overview of the French and Indian War. Here you will learn about the causes of the war and the outcome. You will also find a link to the Paris Peace Treaty of 1763.

Link to this Internet site from http://www.myreportlinks.com

▶**George Washington: The Soldier through the French and Indian War**

This site relates the story of George Washington's role in the French and Indian War. Washington's attack on a French force in May 1754 is said to have started the war in the Americas.

Link to this Internet site from http://www.myreportlinks.com

▶**History: Wars: Seven Years' War**

This brief entry explains the relationship between the French and Indian War and the Seven Years' War. The latter began officially on May 15, 1756, when Britain declared war on France.

Link to this Internet site from http://www.myreportlinks.com

▶**Introduction to the Diaries of George Washington**

At this Web site you can learn all about George Washington from his diaries. Here you will find accounts of Washington's experiences in the French and Indian War.

Link to this Internet site from http://www.myreportlinks.com

▶**Jeffrey Amherst and Small Pox Blankets**

At this Web site you will learn about Jeffrey Amherst's legacy and involvement in the French and Indian War. You will also learn that Amherst discussed tactics to give small pox infected blankets to American Indians, hoping the disease would weaken them.

Link to this Internet site from http://www.myreportlinks.com

▶**The Philadelphia Print Shop Ltd.: The French & Indian War, 1754–63**

This site showcases a number of period maps of the regions contested during the French and Indian War. This commercial site features images of the original maps, all of which can be purchased from the site.

Link to this Internet site from http://www.myreportlinks.com

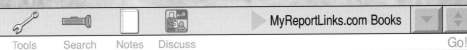

Report Links

The Internet sites described below can be accessed at
**http://www.myreportlinks.com**

▶**The Point: William Pitt**
At this Web site you will find a biography of William Pitt, who was in
charge of military affairs and colonial policy during the French and
Indian War.

Link to this Internet site from http://www.myreportlinks.com

▶**Pontiac's Rebellion**
Pontiac's Rebellion occurred at the end of the French and Indian War.
At this Web site you will learn about the causes and outcome of
this American Indian rebellion.

Link to this Internet site from http://www.myreportlinks.com

▶**Rearview Mirror: Chief Pontiac's Siege of Detroit**
At this site you will learn how Chief Pontiac led warriors from various
American Indian tribes in laying siege to British-held Fort Detroit in
1763. The chief died six years later at the hands of a Peoria tribesman.

Link to this Internet site from http://www.myreportlinks.com

▶**Significant Scots: Robert Dinwiddie**
This site provides a description of Robert Dinwiddie and his
involvement in the French and Indian War. Here you will learn about
how Dinwiddie tried to help the Indians and British colonies in their
fight against the French.

Link to this Internet site from http://www.myreportlinks.com

▶**Welcome to the Oneida Indian Nation Treaty Project**
At this Web site you will find links to important treaties regarding
American Indians. You will also find links to learn about their cultures
and history.

Link to this Internet site from http://www.myreportlinks.com

▶**William Pitt: 1st Earl of Chatham**
At this Web site you will find a brief biography of William Pitt, who in
1757 was called upon to form a governing coalition with Newcastle
during the Seven Years' War.

Link to this Internet site from http://www.myreportlinks.com

## French and Indian War Facts

### ▶ List of Combatants

*North America—The French and Indian War:*
England, American colonists, and a shifting cast of American Indian allies. They fought against France, Canadian colonists, and a shifting cast of American Indian allies.

*Europe—The Seven Years' War:*
England and the German states of Hanover and Prussia. They fought against France, Austria, Russia, Saxony, Spain, and Sweden.

### ▶ Casualties

*Note:* Neither side kept formal records listing the number of dead and wounded. To further complicate matters, casualty lists compiled by French and English officers often report wildly different numbers. Here are the generally accepted casualty figures from two of the war's major battles:

*Battle of the Wilderness (Monongahela) (July 9, 1755):*
England—63 officers killed or wounded; 914 enlisted killed or wounded. France—16 French and Canadian soldiers killed or wounded; American Indians—27 killed or wounded.

*Second Battle of Quebec (April–May, 1759):* England—259 killed, 829 wounded. France—193 killed, 640 wounded.

*Civilian casualties:* Historians estimate that some 2,000 English settlers died or were taken captive by American Indian raiders during the first year of the war—with many more to follow.

### ▶ A Brief Time Line

**1753**—France constructs three forts in the Ohio Valley.

George Washington warns the French to clear out.

**1754**—French troops build Fort Duquesne at the forks of the Ohio.

Washington fires first shots of the war; surrenders Fort Necessity.

**1755**—General Braddock defeated in Battle of the Wilderness (Monongahela).

**1756**—Seven Years' War begins in Europe.

**1757**—William Pitt breathes new life into England's war effort.

**1758**—English capture Fort Louisbourg and Fort Duquesne.

**1759**—English forces win Battle of Quebec.

**1760**—Montreal falls, ending French resistance in Canada.

**1763**—Treaty of Paris formally ends French and Indian War and the Seven Years' War.

# Birth of a Legend

The year was 1753. The British had settled along the Atlantic coast from Massachusetts to South Carolina. Governor Robert Dinwiddie of Virginia should have been content. His peaceful English colony was growing richer with each harvest. Far to the west, however, storm clouds were gathering. The reports piled on his desk told him that the French were moving into the Ohio Valley from Canada. In the face of that threat, the orders from London were clear. If the French refused to withdraw, they must be driven out.

Dinwiddie thought it best to start with a warning. He wrote a letter that advised the French not to settle on lands "known to be the property of the Crown of Great Britain."[1] To deliver the letter he chose a tall militia major, "a person of distinction."[2] Although Major George Washington was only twenty-one, all who knew him said he was both tough and smart. After he picked up his orders, the

George Washington became a ▶ lieutenant colonel at the age of twenty-two.

major assembled a small party of horsemen. It was early November when they set off from Williamsburg, Virginia, for the Ohio Valley. Christopher Gist, a skilled woodsman and a member of the Ohio Company, led the way across the Appalachian Mountains.

## Into the Wilderness

Cold weather and flooded streams slowed progress to a crawl. Undaunted, Major Washington took careful note of all he saw. The forks where the Allegheny and Monongahela rivers merge to form the Ohio River caught his eye. The location, he wrote, is "extreamly well situated for a Fort; as it has the absolute Command of both Rivers."[3] As if in agreement, the French also were planning to build a fort there. Further on, in Logstown, Pennsylvania (present-day Ambridge, Pennsylvania), the Virginians met with Delaware, Shawnee, and Mingo chiefs. Tanaghrisson, a friendly Mingo chief known as Half-King, led the party to the French outpost at Fort Le Boeuf, near Lake Erie.

The fort's French commandant, Captain Jacques Legardeur de Sainte Pierre, greeted his visitors warmly. When he learned the reason for the visit, Legardeur assembled his officers to study Dinwiddie's letter. Then the captain penned a firm reply. "As to the summons you send me to retire," Legardeur wrote, "I do not think myself obliged to obey it."[4] Young Major Washington tucked the letter away and ordered his men to head for home. Legardeur also informed Washington that he would send Dinwiddie's letter on to his superior, the Marquis de Duquesne.

The return trip tested the party's survival skills. One by one the horses gave out, leaving the men afoot in the deep snow. Impatient with the delays, the major told all but Gist to take an easier, slower route. Then, on foot and carrying packs, Washington and Gist started their trek eastward. "The Major was much fatigued," Gist wrote, and the nights were "very cold." The streams were frozen, he added, so that "we could hardly get water to drink."[5]

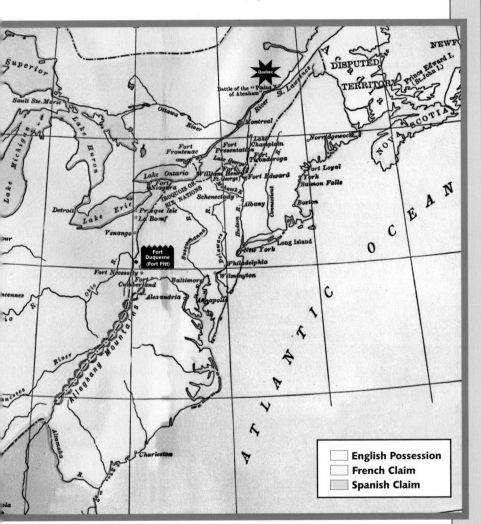

A map of the North American colonies at the time of the French and Indian War. Highlighted are two of the major battlefields, Fort Duquesne and Quebec.

## ▶ Two Close Calls

An American Indian appeared and offered to act as a guide. A few hours later, he revealed his true purpose. As the two Virginians entered a clearing, he wheeled and fired at them. Luckily, the musket ball flew wide. Gist and the major raced forward and tackled the man before he could reload. Gist wanted to kill the treacherous guide, but the major set the man free.

The Virginians hoped to find the Allegheny River frozen solid. Instead, an open channel of icy water barred their way. With the aid of Gist's hatchet they made a crude raft and clambered aboard. As the raft neared midstream, the major's pole caught in the ice and tossed him into the river. Later he wrote, "I fortunately saved my self by catching hold of one of the raft logs."[6] When the raft stuck fast, the men waded to a small island. They awoke the next day with frostbitten toes, but the bitter cold was also an ally. During the night the river had frozen solid. Limping on half-frozen feet, the men stumbled to the far shore.

On December 30, 1753, Gist and the major reached a trader's cabin on Turtle Creek. Once inside, a crackling fire and warm food restored their spirits. Two days later, mounted on borrowed horses, the men reached their homes. At Williamsburg, Virginia, the major delivered Legardeur's letter and turned in his report. Dinwiddie thanked him and turned to his next task. If the French would not listen to warnings, perhaps they would respond to force.

Newspapers rushed the story into print. As the news spread, readers cheered the young Virginian's exploits. Major George Washington had taken a long stride down the path toward becoming an American legend.

# Chapter 2

# Origins of a Wilderness War

The war that would soon sweep across the Ohio Valley was rooted in European rivalries. When the kings of the day spoke, their word was law. Louis XIV of France and George II of England could—and did—start wars with little or no provocation. To enhance their glory and finances, both kings longed for profitable colonies.

By the 1750s, the North American colonies were worth fighting over. French and English settlers shipped tobacco, timber, and other products valued by their countrymen in France and England. Further west, American Indians exchanged pelts for guns, cloth, and beads. With beaver hats all the rage in Europe, each boatload of furs helped fill the royal purse. Control of the Ohio Valley meant continued access to all these products and land for future development.

## ▶ A Global Clash of Interests

England and France were enjoying an uneasy peace when Washington rode westward in 1753. Just eight years earlier, King George's War had spilled over into North America. In one notable campaign, a force of English colonial soldiers won a bloody victory at Fort Louisbourg on Cape Breton Island, Nova Scotia. However, when the war ended in 1748, the peace treaty returned Louisbourg to the French. The colonists grumbled that King George had ignored their sacrifices.[1]

For a time, France seemed to have the upper hand. With Louisbourg restored, French warships controlled the

approaches to the Gulf of St. Lawrence. On land, Louis XIV claimed a tract of land that stretched from Cape Breton Island to the Great Lakes. To the south, a string of French settlements dotted the Mississippi Valley. On the map, this huge territory dwarfed England's Atlantic colonies. That fact angered King George II, who claimed the region—the colonies along the Atlantic coast of America and all the territory west of them—for England.

## ▶ Choosing the Lesser of Two Evils

While France and England argued, the Iroquois Confederacy held sway in the Ohio River valley. The Confederacy protected weaker client nations and crushed opponents. The Five Nations of the Iroquois— the Onondaga, Mohawk, Seneca, Oneida, and Cayuga—invited the Tuscarora to join them as the Six Nations of the Confederacy. The Confederacy was a loose political unit, which had sprung up from the Great League of Peace, a centuries old system the Five Nations had used to settle disputes. The Confederacy was actually weakening by 1752, but its ability to negotiate on behalf of the member nations was still prized.

Neither France nor England worried about the rights of American Indians. As a rule, they kept treaties with the Indian tribes only as long as it was useful to do so. That fact became clear in 1752 at Logstown. A party of Virginians traveled there to meet with the leaders of the Delaware, Shawnee, and Mingo nations. Tanaghrisson, a Catawba by birth, but raised a Mingo, was the spokesperson for the Iroquois League. If all went well, the Virginians hoped to buy tribal lands for resale to settlers. The Virginians began by tempting the chiefs with the promise of cheap trade goods. Next, a spokesman proclaimed,

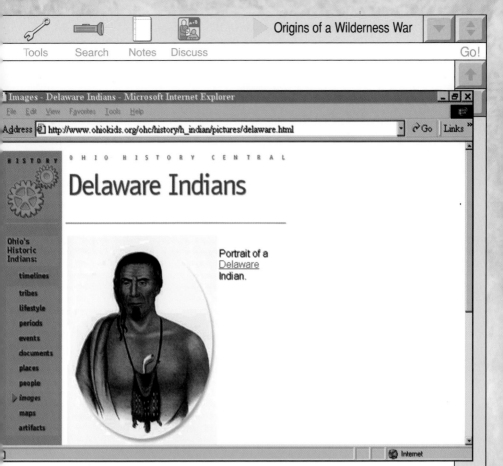

Tools    Search    Notes    Discuss                                    Go!

Images - Delaware Indians - Microsoft Internet Explorer

File   Edit   View   Favorites   Tools   Help

Address   http://www.ohiokids.org/ohc/history/h_indian/pictures/delaware.html      Go   Links

OHIO HISTORY CENTRAL

# Delaware Indians

Ohio's
Historic
Indians:

timelines
tribes
lifestyle
periods
events
documents
places
people
► images
maps
artifacts

Portrait of a
Delaware
Indian.

Internet

▲ The Delaware Indians were one of several tribes that were pushed westward by white settlers.

"Brethren, be assur'd that the King, our Father, by purchasing your Lands, had never any Intention of *takeing them from you*, but that we might live together as one People, and *keep them from the French*, who wou'd be bad Neighbours."[2] The honeyed words failed to ease the fears of these Ohio groups. Like most American Indians, they viewed *all* settlers as "bad neighbors."

To make matters worse, tribes from the southeast and west were moving into the Ohio region. The western tribes wanted to be closer to the white man's trade goods. The

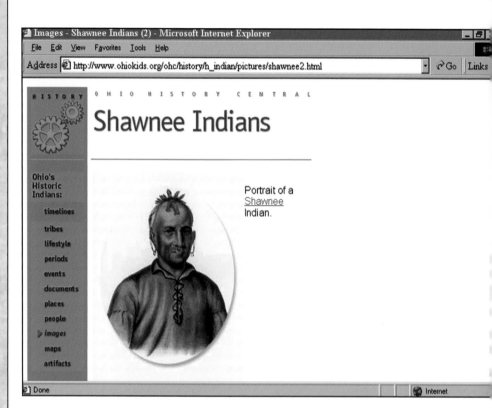

Images - Shawnee Indians (2) - Microsoft Internet Explorer

File   Edit   View   Favorites   Tools   Help

Address  http://www.ohiokids.org/ohc/history/h_indian/pictures/shawnee2.html    Go   Links

HISTORY          OHIO   HISTORY   CENTRAL

# Shawnee Indians

Ohio's
Historic
Indians:

timelines

tribes

lifestyle

periods

events

documents

places

people

▶ images

maps

artifacts

Portrait of a
Shawnee
Indian.

Done                                                    Internet

▲ The Shawnee were one tribe that sided with the French during the French and Indian War.

eastern tribes—Shawnee and Delaware—had little choice. Waves of white settlers were pushing them westward. Some still lived along the Delaware, their home for hundreds of years. In its heyday, the great Iroquois Confederacy might have held the tribes together. Now, it was breaking apart as well.

As the months slipped past, the tribes began to take sides. Many chose the French, who seemed less land-hungry. A smaller number of tribes cast their lot with the English. If war was coming, the tribes wanted to be on the winning side.

## ▶ A Race to Dominate the Ohio Valley

The weight of numbers helped push France and England into conflict. Less than a hundred thousand settlers lived in New France. The thirteen English colonies teemed with well over a million colonists. Cities were filling up and cheap farmland was scarce. Tobacco was a good cash crop, but it soon wore out the soil. Lured by cheap, fertile land, these colonists yearned to settle the Ohio Valley. Back in London, royal ministers dreamed of selling land in the region to raise money. Keeping troops stationed overseas was draining the treasury.[3]

The French made the first move. Since 1752, the Marquis de Duquesne had been building forts along the Ohio River. The key to the system, as Washington had noted, lay at the forks of the Ohio. In the spring of 1754, one of Duquesne's canoe brigades reached the site. To their surprise, Dinwiddie's builders had arrived first. The new-comers did not hesitate. With guns at the ready, the French gave the Virginians two choices. They could leave—or be blown to bits. The outnumbered colonists were no fools. They marched away, leaving the French to start work on Fort Duquesne (in present-day Pittsburgh, Pennsylvania).[4]

# War Clouds Gather

The Marquis de Duquesne was the driving force behind the French fort builders. Heedless of the cost, the governor plunged ahead with his grand design. His first strong-points popped up at Presque Isle (Erie, Pennsylvania) and French Creek in western Pennsylvania. The work bogged down at Fort Le Boeuf (Waterford, Pennsylvania), where drought brought canoe travel to a halt. The sight of the large, well-armed brigades awed the Ohio tribes. The Iroquois watched and wondered how the English would react. The Delaware took jobs as porters and guides. Instead of money, they took their pay in trade goods.[1]

## ▶ Dinwiddie Responds to the Threat

Reports of Duquesne's fort building alarmed the English colonists. In Virginia, Governor Dinwiddie wrestled with the French challenge. A letter from an Ohio Company trader spelled out the danger:

> By the last account I can get . . . the French told the Indians their Army when collected will make up 15,000 Men, that . . . [they] have built two Forts down the Ohio, that the Country belongs to them & that they will build when they like.[2]

Like Duquesne, Dinwiddie needed forts to hold the territory. He also hoped to protect his fellow land speculators in the Ohio Company of Virginia. The Virginia House of Burgesses (their legislature) had granted a group of land speculators a third of a million acres on the Ohio River in 1745. The land had been acquired through the Treaty of Lancaster, Pennsylvania, in 1744. In the treaty, the Iroquois Confederacy ceded all its remaining land claims within the boundaries of Maryland and Virginia. Canasatego, the Onondaga leader who negotiated on behalf of the Confederacy, thought this meant the land of the Shenandoah Valley, not the entire Ohio Country. The Virginia commissioners never mentioned that according to the colony's original charter, Virginia extended all the way to the Pacific Ocean.

Back in London, the king's ministers had approved Dinwiddie's plan to fortify the Forks of the Ohio River. They also ordered Dinwiddie to drive out the French if

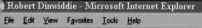

Robert Dinwiddie - Microsoft Internet Explorer

File   Edit   View   Favorites   Tools   Help

Address   http://www.electricscotland.com/history/other/robert_dinwiddie.htm    Go   Links

### Lt. Governor Robert Dinwiddie

Robert Dinwiddie was born of an old Scottish family. His father was a prosperous merchant, and his mother also came from a commercial family. Robert was educated at the University of Glasgow and entered his father's countinghouse. He later carried on a successful carreer as a merchant..

Dinwiddie's role as a colonial administrator began in 1721, when he was appointed British representative in Bermuda. After 16 years of service in Bermuda, he received the important position of surveyor genal, which included jurisdiction over Pennsylvania and the southern colonis of British North America. By tradition the surveyor general was entitled to a seat on the Virginia Council, a post Dinwiddie insisted on assuming. Characteristic of Dinwiddie's service in the Colonies was his zealous attention to the offices under his authority and a tendency to maximize his position by emphasizing the royal prerogative. In recognition of these qualities, he was appointed lieutenant governor of Virginia, England's largest colony, and took office on July 4, 1751.

As lieutenant governor, Dinwiddie saw the beginnings of the conflict on Virginia's fronties that led to the French and Indian War. He was a firm advocate of British expansion into the west. He sought the help of the Indians and the other British colonies in the struggle against the French, pressed the legislature for defense funds, and favored the use of regular armed forces in place of the less reliable militia. Dinwiddie made George Washington a lieutenant colonel in 1754.

Generally, Dinwiddie was able to work in harmony with the Virginia Legislature. He did, however, prompt a serious conflict with the House of Burgess shortly after he took office. In hope of increasing

Done     Internet

▲ *Robert Dinwiddie was lieutenant governor of Virginia from 1751 to 1758. During the French and Indian War, he urged the colonies to help the English drive the French from the Ohio Valley.*

they showed up. To arm the fort, they supplied cannon, shot, and powder.

The governor had begun his campaign by sending Washington to give the French fair warning. Their refusal sent him to the Virginia Assembly. There, "with great Persuasions, many Argum'ts and much difficulty," he won his case. The members voted to allot £10,000 to defend the western lands.[3] His next step was to promote Washington to lieutenant colonel. Early in April 1754, Colonel Washington led 160 ill-trained soldiers into the woods. His orders were to defend the men who were working at the Forks.

## Bloodshed Begins

Washington was nearing the Forks when Tanaghrisson's scouts stopped him. A small French unit, the scouts said, was camped nearby. Fearing a surprise attack, Washington chose to strike first. Leaving the main force to guard his camp, he led forty soldiers on a night march. The Virginians reached the Mingo camp at sunrise after stumbling for hours along a muddy trail. From there, two warriors led them to a rocky hollow. Deep in the shadows, the French troops were just waking up.

The startled soldiers reached for their guns when they spotted the advancing colonists. Suddenly, a volley of musket fire shattered the silence. One ball struck Ensign Joseph Coulon de Jumonville, the French commander. Tanaghrisson raced in, smashed Jumonville's skull, and scalped the young officer. By then the shooting had stopped. Ten Frenchmen and one Virginian lay dead. Washington had won a skirmish—and started the French and Indian War.

Later, each side blamed the other for shooting first. Washington said his men starting shooting because the French were about to fire. In his report, the future general added, "I heard the bullets whistle, and, believe me, there is something charming in the sound."[4] The French argued that Jumonville had come with a warning for the English. He was trying to read out the message when he was shot in cold blood, they said.[5] Which version is closer to the truth? No one can be certain.

## Surrender at Fort Necessity

Washington learned that a larger French force was approaching. He led his men to the Great Meadows and spent three days digging in. Their efforts produced a system of shallow trenches and log ramparts they called Fort Necessity. Low on supplies and powder, the Virginians steeled themselves for an assault. On July 3, Coulon de Villiers, brother of the slain Jumonville, occupied the high ground above the fort. The battle began as his nine hundred men and their American Indian allies fired into the fort's entrenchments.

Rain fell throughout the day. The Virginians stood knee deep in mud and tried to make every shot count. Anyone who poked his head above the ramparts drew a volley of musket fire. As night fell, Villiers offered the colonists a chance to surrender. Washington argued over the terms, but knew he was beaten. Around midnight, he signed the paper that allowed him to lead his men back to Virginia. In his report he listed his losses as 12 killed and 43 wounded. The French admitted to 20 casualties. Neither side mentioned the losses suffered by their American Indian allies.

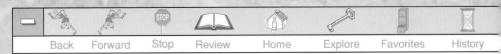
The retreat to Virginia was a nightmare. Left without horses or medicine, the men had to carry their sick and wounded. Washington kept morale high and led his bedraggled troops to safety. The French flag now flew from the Allegheny Mountains to the Mississippi River.[6]

## Plans for a Wider War

Dinwiddie praised Washington despite the setback. He blamed the loss of Fort Necessity on a lack of manpower and urged the colonies to strike back. The Ohio Company added its voice to the call to battle. Until the French were driven out, the partners could not claim their 200,000-acre land grant. While Dinwiddie raised money and troops, other governors wooed the Ohio tribes. The chiefs accepted their gifts—but would not promise to fight for King George II.

In London, two regiments of British soldiers, the famed Redcoats, were setting sail for America. General Edward Braddock led these fresh, well-trained troops.

# Frontier Warfare

**E**arly in 1755, England and France prepared to fight for the North American lands each claimed as its own. Both nations drew up battle plans, even though neither had declared war. To men fighting in the woods, the war was quite real—and often fatal.

In April, General Braddock, who had arrived in Virginia from London, held a council of war. Among the colonial governors who met in Alexandria were Dinwiddie of Virginia, Robert Morris of Pennsylvania, William Shirley of Massachusetts, Horatio Sharpe of Maryland, James DeLancey of New York, and Arthur Dobbs of North Carolina. The council agreed to launch a four-pronged attack.

Braddock chose Fort Duquesne as his objective. The forts at Lake George, Nova Scotia, and Niagara would also be targeted. The French had controlled Niagara since the late 1600s, but this did not trouble the English. Their goal was to drive the French from soil they claimed as their own.[1]

Each side did its best to enlist American Indian tribes as allies. Tribal leaders, for the most part, favored the French. The chiefs told Christian Post as much when he met with them. Post, a lay missionary, was one of the rare colonists who admired the native culture. He had a facility for learning American Indian languages quickly. Although he argued that the English wanted trade, not land, his listeners shook their heads. The chiefs asked, "Why do you [and the French] come to fight on our land? This makes

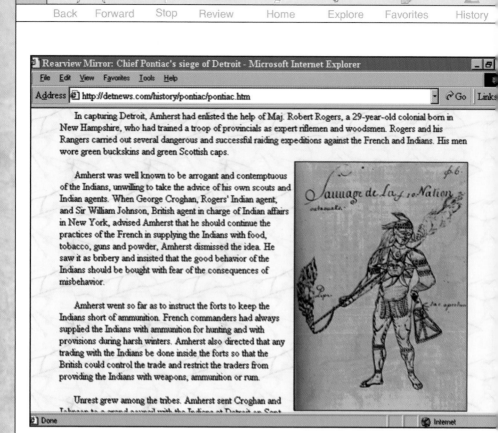

In capturing Detroit, Amherst had enlisted the help of Maj. Robert Rogers, a 29-year-old colonial born in New Hampshire, who had trained a troop of provincials as expert riflemen and woodsmen. Rogers and his Rangers carried out several dangerous and successful raiding expeditions against the French and Indians. His men wore green buckskins and green Scottish caps.

Amherst was well known to be arrogant and contemptuous of the Indians, unwilling to take the advice of his own scouts and Indian agents. When George Croghan, Rogers' Indian agent, and Sir William Johnson, British agent in charge of Indian affairs in New York, advised Amherst that he should continue the practices of the French in supplying the Indians with food, tobacco, guns and powder, Amherst dismissed the idea. He saw it as bribery and insisted that the good behavior of the Indians should be bought with fear of the consequences of misbehavior.

Amherst went so far as to instruct the forts to keep the Indians short of ammunition. French commanders had always supplied the Indians with ammunition for hunting and with provisions during harsh winters. Amherst also directed that any trading with the Indians be done inside the forts so that the British could control the trade and restrict the traders from providing the Indians with weapons, ammunition or rum.

Unrest grew among the tribes. Amherst sent Croghan and

▲ *This sketch of an American Indian warrior was done by a Frenchman.*

every body believe, you want to take the land from us by force, and settle it."[2] Only a respect for English power kept more tribes from joining the French.

## ▶ Battle of the Wilderness

The campaign to capture Fort Duquesne began slowly. Braddock needed wagons and supplies, but the colonists ignored his pleas. At that point, the well-respected Ben Franklin stepped forward. The army, he warned, would take by force what was not given freely. Only then did Pennsylvania's farmers furnish Braddock with horses and wagons. Franklin also noted the bad feelings that English troops aroused in their colonial cousins. He wrote that the Redcoats "plundered and stripped the inhabitants . . . besides insulting, abusing, and confining the people if they [protested]."[3]

At last, on June 10, 1775, Braddock gave the orders to march. George Washington rode beside him as an aide. In time, the general learned to trust the young Virginian's common-sense advice. It was too late, however, to add American Indians to the army. Years of broken promises had turned the Delaware and Shawnee against the English. Most of the fifty warriors who did join the march soon drifted away. As Chief Scarouady complained, "[Braddock] looked upon us as dogs, and would never hear anything that we said to him."[4]

With three hundred axmen clearing the way, the column lumbered forward. To speed the advance, Washington suggested they leave the heavy baggage behind. An impatient Braddock agreed. Moving faster now, the force of 1,200 regular and militia soldiers closed in on Fort Duquesne. To guard against ambush, a strong advance guard marched ahead of the main body. The unit had just crossed a wide ravine when lookouts saw a French scout stop and wave his hat. The signal touched off a barrage of fire from hidden riflemen. The Battle of the Wilderness (also called Monongahela) had begun.

The Redcoats looked in vain for targets. Using wilderness tactics, their attackers were firing from deep cover. Commands rang out and the trained English troops moved to the attack. As one man they screamed, "God save the King!" Still yelling, they swept forward, stopping only to fire and reload. The sight of the oncoming Redcoats spooked the French militia. Many of them broke and ran.

Still fighting by the book—in long lines, one behind the other—the English loaded their cannon and fired. Smoke swirled as cannon balls crashed through the trees.

The tide of battle turned in the next instant. A sharp volley from French regulars halted the advance. Then, as if on cue, American Indian warriors allied with the French renewed their attack. Whooping as they fired, their bullets shredded the Redcoat line. Confused and panicked by the war cries, the troops tried to flee. As they did so, they collided with Braddock's main body. The two units became badly tangled. Only the Virginia militiamen took cover and returned the incoming fire. They might have beaten off the attack, but the Redcoats were shooting at anything that moved. Caught in a crossfire, the colonists had to withdraw.

With the battle lost, Braddock ordered a retreat. As he did so, a bullet shattered his arm and punctured a lung. Washington had two horses killed under him. Later, he counted four bullet holes in his uniform. As the beaten army limped away, the French retired to the fort. The American Indians swarmed onto the killing field to take scalps.

The beaten army burned what could not be carried away. Braddock died the next day, adding to the long casualty list. Of his 86 officers, 63 had been killed or wounded. Of 1,373 enlisted men, 914 suffered the same fate. By contrast, the French lost only 16 men. Their American Indian allies, who did much of the fighting, suffered 27 casualties.[5]

## ▶ Hopeful Signs Amid the Gloom

Braddock's defeat dealt English hopes a severe setback. As the news spread, more tribes stepped forward to fight beside the French. At sea, Duquesne's cargo ships slipped past the Royal Navy's blockade. On land, the French

Tools    Search    Notes    Discuss    Go!

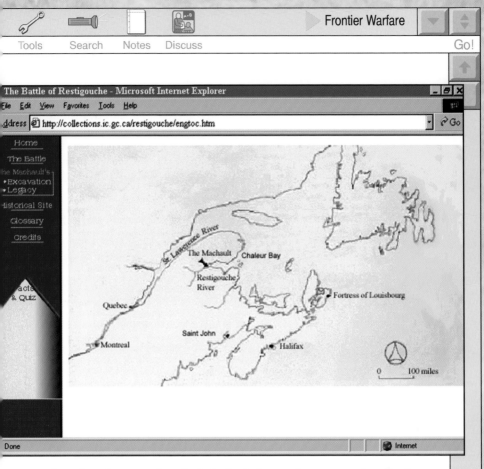

The Battle of Restigouche - Microsoft Internet Explorer

File  Edit  View  Favorites  Tools  Help

Address  http://collections.ic.gc.ca/restigouche/engtoc.htm    Go

Home
The Battle
The Machault's
• Excavation
• Legacy
Historical Site
Glossary
Credits

Facts
& Quiz

Done    Internet

▲ *Before they were forced off the land, the Acadians occupied much of the area from Saint John to the Fortress of Louisbourg.*

stocked their forts with supplies left behind each time the English withdrew. One retreat came after Governor William Shirley of Massachusetts called off his attack on Niagara. Adding to the gloom, the tobacco crop failed because of drought.

The English did see a few hopeful signs. In June 1755, a force of colonists overran Fort Beauséjour in Nova Scotia. The victors then turned to the Nova Scotia peninsula's French settlers. Fearing a revolt, the English forced the Acadians, the name given to the French settlers, to leave their homes. Many migrated to Louisiana, where

they gave birth to Cajun culture. Sir William Johnson fought well at Lake George, but his campaign ended in a stalemate. In London, seizing on this glimmer of good news, Parliament awarded Johnson a princely £5,000.[6]

Johnson wore many hats and yielded much authority in colonial America. Through his "excellent English political connections and influential positions on the New York frontier (Mohawk Valley merchant, colonel of militia, army contractor, great land speculator . . . )," he amassed a great fortune. Beginning in 1755, he served for nearly twenty years as the British superintendent of Northern Indian affairs.[7]

# Turn of the Tide

The war that began in North America soon spread across the globe. England and France fought for empire in the Americas, Europe, and India. England's allies included the German states of Prussia and Hanover. France counted Spain, Austria, Russia, Sweden, and Saxony as partners.

▲ Sir William Pitt was a bold leader who was picked to lead the English forces during the French and Indian War. He is perhaps most remembered for finding the bright young officers who led the British troops to victory.

History books refer to the conflict as the Seven Years' War (1754–63).

King George II looked for—and found—a bold new leader in Sir William Pitt, a member of the House of Commons. Pitt breathed new life into the war effort after he took charge in 1757. If England wished to expand its empire, Pitt knew it must defeat France in North America. Soon more troops, ships, and supplies were flowing to the colonies. To provide fresh leadership, Pitt promoted several bright young colonels. Then he told his new generals to carry "the War into the Heart of the Enemy's Possessions."[1]

▲ The Battle at Fort Louisbourg was a major turning point in the war.

## Return to Louisbourg

Pitt's first target was Fort Louisbourg. A victory there would open the St. Lawrence pathway to the French capital of Quebec. Colonial troops had captured the Cape Breton Island stronghold in 1745, only to see it returned to France. Now, three thousand French soldiers manned the fort. In the harbor, twelve warships lay at anchor. On June 1, 1758, the garrison watched as an English fleet sailed into view.

General Jeffrey Amherst led the invasion force. The daring James Wolfe ranked as second in command to Amherst. Wolfe tried to make a forced landing at Freshwater Cove on June 8, 1758, only to be driven off by the dug-in defenders. Sheltered by a rocky point, three of his boats did manage to reach the shore. Wolfe quickly ordered his main force to follow. Boats overturned and men drowned in the heavy surf, but still Wolfe urged his troops on. Once they reached the beach, the Redcoats regrouped and routed the defenders.

The English now had the French caught in a vise. In the harbor, naval gunfire hit the warship *Célèbre* and started a fire.[2] Windblown flames quickly spread to the sails of two more warships. Amherst's soldiers, firing from newly dug trenches, raked Louisbourg with musket fire. Inside the walls, morale sagged as hospital beds filled with wounded. On July 26, to prevent further bloodshed, Louisbourg's governor, the Chevalier de Drucour, agreed to surrender.[3] Pitt's generals had won their first great victory.

## Return to Fort Duquesne

The tide of war was swinging, but the French were still full of fight. A few weeks before, British General James

Abercrombie had led 12,000 soldiers against Fort Ticonderoga. The 3,000 defenders, led by the Marquis de Montcalm, crushed the head-on assault. When the news reached London, an angry Pitt replaced Abercrombie with Jeffrey Amherst.[4]

Further south, American Indian raiders were burning British colonial settlements. George Washington did his best to guard the frontier, but it was an impossible task. Eventually he was recalled from his Loyalhanna Creek camp to join General John Forbes for a new thrust at Fort Duquesne. Washington and his troops advanced quickly to the Forks where he was to join Forbes. Forbes, on the other hand, proceeded slowly and deliberately from Carlisle, Pennsylvania. He carved out a route that would later become known as Forbes Road—a path with way stations approximately two miles apart, connecting Philadelphia with the Ohio Valley. Weakened by dysentery, Forbes traveled in a litter slung between two horses. Day after day he jolted over a road his axmen hacked through the woods. Forbes described the route as "overgrown everywhere with trees and brushwood, so that nowhere can one see twenty yards."[5]

The fort's defenders were badly outnumbered. Their numbers dwindled further as the Shawnee and Mingo allies of the French slipped away. In September, the French bought some time by mauling an advance party of English troops. Forbes, intent on his road building, refused to quicken his pace. That changed in November, when his men brought in three French prisoners. The French garrison, the captives said, numbered only a few hundred men. Pushing forward with 2,500 of his best troops, Forbes set up camp a day's march from the fort. That night the men heard explosions in the distance. When they reached the

Forks the next day, they found a deserted ruin. The French had evacuated the few remaining troops and destroyed the fort. The city of Pittsburgh would one day rise from those ashes. In 1758, the victory meant that England had gained control of the western frontier.[6]

## ▶ Final Campaigns: Quebec and Montreal

In the spring of 1759, two English forces menaced Quebec. Amherst led the main force through the Hudson River valley, heading toward Lake Champlain. The cautious Amherst advanced slowly, "perfecting his defenses" as he moved. Wolfe led a smaller force on a more direct route up the St. Lawrence. When he reached Quebec in late June, he turned his ships' guns on the city. Inside his

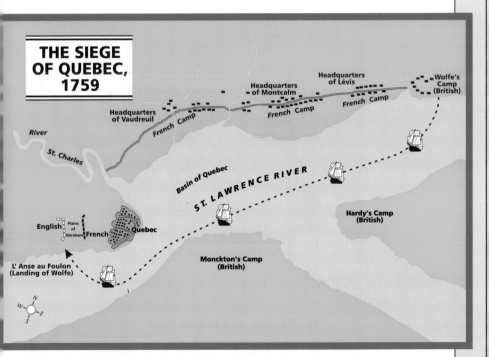

**THE SIEGE OF QUEBEC, 1759**

General James Wolfe sailed to Quebec in June 1759. He was finally able to lead an attack on the well-fortified city in September.

fortress, perched high above the city, the Marquis de Montcalm studied his maps. The charts showed that Quebec was well guarded by steep cliffs.

Weeks passed as the English searched for a way to scale the cliffs that lined the river. At last Wolfe found a path up the western cliffs. Early on September 13, the first troops climbed what Montcalm thought was an "impossible" bluff.[7] By morning, over four thousand Redcoats stood in battle array on the nearby Plains of Abraham. The astonished Montcalm marched his army down to the plains and ordered an attack. The motley force of French regulars, woodsmen, and farmers rushed forward, firing as they

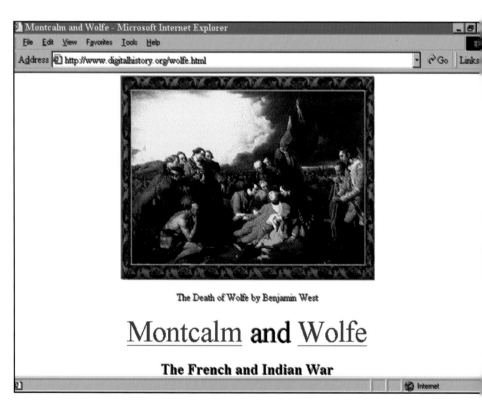

James Wolfe was the British general whose success in the Battle of Quebec won Canada for the British Empire.

came. The English troops stood fast, muskets ready. As men fell, others stepped up to take their places.

The Frenchmen closed to forty paces and still the Redcoats held their fire. Finally, Wolfe barked the order. Flintlocks snapped and a hail of musket balls tore the French line to shreds. Then, bayonets fixed, the Redcoats drove the survivors back to the city gates. Both Montcalm and Wolfe were among the casualties. Quebec surrendered four days later.

With its supply lines cut, Montreal now dangled like a fruit ripe for picking. Canadian militiamen had long since deserted. American Indians were withdrawing their support from both sides. Generals Amherst, Murray, and Haviland reached Montreal within days of each other. Amherst had planned well.

In the face of Amherst's superior strength, Governor-General Vaudreuil gave up the city of Montreal without a fight. On September 9, 1760, the two men exchanged signed copies of a surrender agreement. The war in North America between France and England—and their allies— was over. As historian Francis Parkman writes, "Half the continent had changed hands at the stroke of a pen."[8]

# Chapter 6

# Prelude to Revolution

**T**he English victory in North America did not end the war in Europe. Both sides were exhausted, but still their armies clawed at each other. Peace came when England's George III took his grandfather's place on the throne. Eager to end the costly war with France and her major allies, the new king loosened his ties with Prussia, which was at war with Austria. The move freed George III to make peace

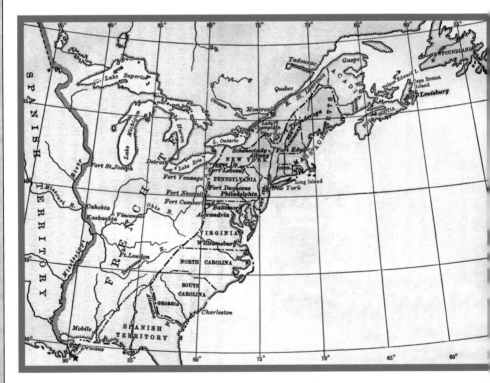

▲ After the French and Indian War the British gained all French and Spanish possessions east of the Mississippi. The green area is the land that Britain controlled prior to the war.

with France. In 1763, the warring nations signed the Treaty of Paris.

The treaty awarded England a large portion of North America. France gave up its claims to the lands east of the Mississippi, and Spain gave up Florida. As payment for losing Florida (the territory stretching from Georgia to the Mississippi River), Spain was given Louisiana. At that time, the Louisiana Territory included all of the former French lands west of the Mississippi. France kept only two small islands off Newfoundland as ports for its fishing fleet.

## ▶ Pontiac's Rebellion

No one consulted the American Indians about these massive land transfers. A number of tribes had switched sides to fight beside the English, but the alliances did not last. The tribes were angered by the collapse of the Treaty of Easton. In that 1758 agreement, Pennsylvania had promised to close the lands west of the Alleghenies to settlement. After the fall of Fort Duquesne, settlers had flooded in despite the treaty. General Jeffrey Amherst terminated customary gift distributions to the American Indians as well. As a Cayuga chief had warned, "I fear [the English] only speak from their Mouth, and not from their Heart."[1]

The arrival of new settlers touched off a frontier war in 1763. Chief Pontiac of the Ottawa organized the Ohio Valley tribes into a confederation. In May, as Pontiac had planned, each group attacked a nearby English fort. Eight outposts fell to the attackers. Entire garrisons were massacred. Pontiac led the assault on Detroit, but failed to overrun the fort. He then carried out a five-month siege that was broken by the arrival of fresh British troops. The rebellion sputtered out after Pontiac signed a peace treaty in 1766.

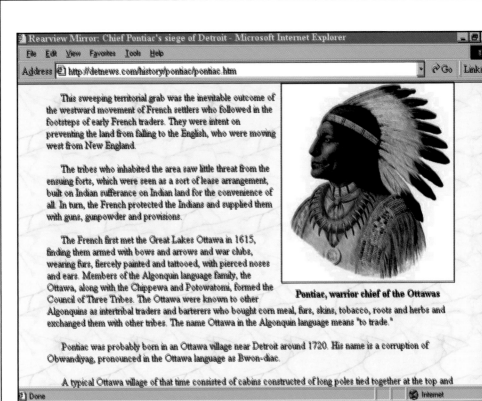

Rearview Mirror: Chief Pontiac's siege of Detroit - Microsoft Internet Explorer

File Edit View Favorites Tools Help

Address http://detnews.com/history/pontiac/pontiac.htm — Go Links

This sweeping territorial grab was the inevitable outcome of the westward movement of French settlers who followed in the footsteps of early French traders. They were intent on preventing the land from falling to the English, who were moving west from New England.

The tribes who inhabited the area saw little threat from the ensuing forts, which were seen as a sort of lease arrangement, built on Indian sufferance on Indian land for the convenience of all. In turn, the French protected the Indians and supplied them with guns, gunpowder and provisions.

The French first met the Great Lakes Ottawa in 1615, finding them armed with bows and arrows and war clubs, wearing furs, fiercely painted and tattooed, with pierced noses and ears. Members of the Algonquin language family, the Ottawa, along with the Chippewa and Potowatomi, formed the Council of Three Tribes. The Ottawa were known to other Algonquins as intertribal traders and barterers who bought corn meal, furs, skins, tobacco, roots and herbs and exchanged them with other tribes. The name Ottawa in the Algonquin language means "to trade."

**Pontiac, warrior chief of the Ottawas**

Pontiac was probably born in an Ottawa village near Detroit around 1720. His name is a corruption of Obwandiyag, pronounced in the Ottawa language as Bwon-diac.

A typical Ottawa village of that time consisted of cabins constructed of long poles tied together at the top and

Done — Internet

Chief Pontiac of the Ottawa organized the Ohio Valley tribes into a confederation.

## Colonial Reactions

Years of fighting alongside British officers and regular troops had not endeared the colonists to their British "cousins." Now at home again with their families these colonists were still not entirely happy. One complaint focused on the plan to keep a large army in the colonies. London claimed that the troops were there to protect frontier settlements. Few believed that story. Most thought the army's mission was to make sure the colonies stayed loyal. A friend in London summed it up for Benjamin Franklin.

"The army's purpose," he said, was "to preserve a Military Awe over you."[2]

By 1763, many colonists thought and spoke of themselves as Americans. Peace did little to improve colonial relations with England. Had their militia not fought alongside the boastful Redcoats and outmarched and outfought them on many occasions? Highborn English officers, the colonists complained, treated them with contempt.[3] To make matters worse, Parliament wanted the colonists to pay for the upkeep of the British soldiers. They said they were required to protect British citizens—in this case the American colonists—so far from England. The Stamp Act of 1763 ignited the colonists' smoldering resentment. Without the hated stamps, no contract or deed was legal. Violators were tried without juries. Up and down the Atlantic Coast, Americans protested the tax. Merchants refused to buy English goods. Courts closed rather than use the stamps. Street mobs threatened to tar and feather the tax collectors. As the unrest spread, British troops marched into the cities to enforce the law. The repeal of the Stamp Act a year later did not end the unrest. Americans began to talk openly of revolution.

## ▶ A Future Commanding General

The man destined to lead that revolution was busy at his Mount Vernon estate. George Washington was no longer the young hothead who had fought the first battle of the French and Indian War. On the battlefield he had earned respect for his courage and sound judgment. Back in camp, he handled the headaches of recruitment and supply with a skill born of hard-won experience.[4] His fellow officers told him as much when he bid them farewell. Their letter expressed sorrow for the loss of

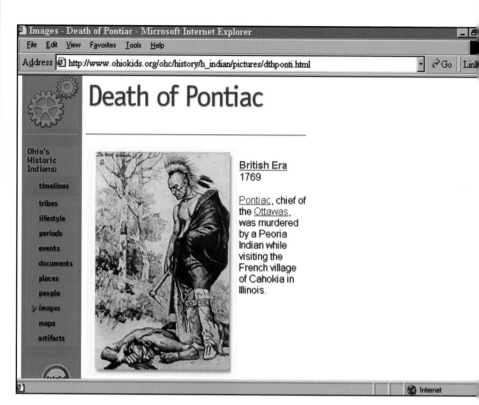

# Death of Pontiac

**British Era**
1769

Pontiac, chief of the Ottawas, was murdered by a Peoria Indian while visiting the French village of Cahokia in Illinois.

Ohio's Historic Indians:

- timelines
- tribes
- lifestyle
- periods
- events
- documents
- places
- people
- images
- maps
- artifacts

▲ Pontiac was murdered by a Peoria Indian in 1769.

"such an excellent commander, such a sincere friend, and so affable a companion."[5]

Washington was deeply rooted in his native soil. He built up Mount Vernon and brought Martha Custis to live there after their marriage. To stay involved in public affairs, he won a seat in Virginia's House of Burgesses. Passage of the Stamp Act struck him as "ill-judged" and likely "unconstitutional."[6] When the First Continental Congress met in 1774, Washington agreed with its Declaration of Rights. Americans, he wrote, would never "submit to the loss of those valuable rights and privileges which are essential to the happiness of every free state."[7]

Tools     Search     Notes     Discuss     Go!

On June 15, 1775, a new nation called him to lead its armed forces. Washington accepted the task with his usual modesty. In a brief address, he declared that he "would exert every power I possess" on behalf of the "Glorious cause."[8] Eight days later he headed north to Boston, enroute to becoming the first military hero of the Revolutionary War.

*Note: Throughout this book all quoted excerpts appear as in the original writing, except where indicated. At the time of the French and Indian War, the spelling and punctuation rules in effect today were not yet established or universally practiced, thus there are grammatical errors in several quotes. It may also be that some individuals were not skilled in grammar and spelling.*

## Chapter 1. Birth of a Legend

1. Francis Jennings, *Empire of Fortune* (New York: W. W. Norton & Company, 1988), p. 62.

2. John R. Alden, *George Washington: A Biography* (Baton Rouge: Louisiana State University Press, 1984), p. 16.

3. Donald Jackson, ed., "Journey to the French Commandant 31 October 1753–16 January 1754," *The Diaries of George Washington, Vol. I* (Charlottesville: University Press of Virginia, 1976), <http://memory.loc.gov /ammem/gwhtml/gwseries1.html> (June 24, 2001).

4. Ibid.

5. Alden, p. 20.

6. Ibid., p. 21.

## Chapter 2. Origins of a Wilderness War

1. Arthur M. Schlesinger, Jr., ed., *The Almanac of American History* (New York: Barnes & Noble Books, 1993), pp. 88–89.

2. Francis Jennings, *Empire of Fortune* (New York: W. W. Norton & Company, 1988), pp. 39–40.

3. Fred Anderson, *Crucible of War: The Seven Years' War and the Fate of Empire in British North America, 1754–1766* (New York: Alfred A. Knopf, 2000), p. 17.

4. Ibid., pp. 47–49.

## Chapter 3. War Clouds Gather

1. Francis Jennings, *Empire of Fortune* (New York: W. W. Norton & Company, 1988), pp. 51–53.

2. Donald Jackson, ed., Dorothy Twohig, assoc. ed., *The Diaries of George Washington, 1748–65, Vol. I* (Charlottesville: University Press of Virginia, 1975), p. 123.

3. Jennings, p. 65.

4. John R. Alden, *George Washington: A Biography* (Baton Rouge: Louisiana State University Press, 1984), p. 27.

5. Jackson, p. 196.

6. Francis Parkman, *The Seven Years War: A Narrative Taken from Montcalm and Wolfe, The Conspiracy of Pontiac, and A Half-Century of Conflict* (New York: Harper Torchbooks, 1968), p. 68.

Chapter 4. Frontier Warfare

1. Francis Parkman, *The Seven Years War: A Narrative Taken from Montcalm and Wolfe, The Conspiracy of Pontiac, and A Half-Century of Conflict* (New York: Harper Torchbooks, 1968), pp. 78–79.

2. Fred Anderson, *Crucible of War: The Seven Years' War and the Fate of Empire in British North America, 1754–1766* (New York: Alfred A. Knopf, 2000), p. 271.

3. Francis Jennings, *Empire of Fortune* (New York: W. W. Norton & Company, 1988), p. 206.

4. Parkman, p. 83.

5. Ibid., p. 88.

6. Jennings, p. 164.

7. Anderson, p. 81.

Chapter 5. Turn of the Tide

1. Fred Anderson, *Crucible of War: The Seven Years' War and the Fate of Empire in British North America, 1754–1766* (New York: Alfred A. Knopf, 2000), p. 310.

2. Francis Parkman, *The Seven Years War: A Narrative Taken from Montcalm and Wolfe, The Conspiracy of Pontiac, and A Half-Century of Conflict* (New York: Harper Torchbooks, 1968), pp. 176–182.

3. Parkman, p. 179.

4. Arthur M. Schlesinger, Jr., ed., *The Almanac of American History* (New York: Barnes & Noble, 1993), pp. 94–95.

5. Parkman, p. 201.

6. Ibid., p. 206.

7. Francis Jennings, *Empire of Fortune* (New York: W. W. Norton & Company, 1988), p. 423.

8. Parkman, p. 286.

**Chapter 6. Prelude to Revolution**

1. Francis Jennings, *Empire of Fortune* (New York: W. W. Norton & Company, 1988), pp. 399–400.

2. Ibid., p. 460.

3. Harrison Bird, *Battle for a Continent: The French and Indian War 1754–1763* (New York: Oxford University Press, 1965), p. 351.

4. "George Washington," *Ames Laboratory* n.d., <http://sc94.ameslab.gov/TOUR/gwash.html> (June 24, 2001).

5. John R. Alden, *George Washington: A Biography* (Baton Rouge: Louisiana State University Press, 1984), p. 70.

6. Ibid., p. 95.

7. Ibid., p. 105.

8. Ibid., p. 113.

## Further Reading

Bearor, Bob. *French & Indian War Battlesites: A Controversy.* Bowie, Md.: Heritage Books, Inc., 2000.

Brown, Thomas. T*he Narrative of Thomas Brown.* Sharon, Mass.: Ye Galleon Press, 1995.

Collier, Christopher and James Lincoln Collier. *The French and Indian War: 1660–1763.* New York: Benchmark Books, 1998.

Gaines, Ann Graham. *King George III.* Broomall, Pa.: Chelsea House Publishers, 2001.

Leckie, Robert. *A Few Acres of Snow: The Saga of the French and Indian Wars.* New York: John Wiley & Sons, 1999.

Maestro, Betsy. *Struggle for a Continent: The French and Indian Wars, 1689–1763.* New York: Lothrop, Lee & Shepard Books, 1999.

Marrin, Albert. *Struggle for a Continent: The French & Indian Wars, 1690–1760.* New York: Atheneum Books for Young Readers, 1987.

Meltzer, Milton. *The American Revolutionaries: A History in Their Own Words, 1750–1800.* New York: Thomas Y. Crowell, 1987.

Minks, Benton. *The French & Indian War.* San Diego, Calif.: Lucent Books, 1994.

Schwartz, Seymour I. *The French and Indian War, 1754–1763: The Imperial Struggle for North America.* New York: Simon & Schuster, 1994.

## Index